DOMINATE META'S COURSE

THE ADVANCED DEVELOPERS BLUEPRINT FOR MASTERY

LIAM HENRY JR

Table of Contents

Chapter 10.3: Hands-on Exercises (Exploratory)

Preface

Unleashing the Power of Llama: A Comprehensive Guide

The advent of large language models (LLMs) marks a pivotal moment in the evolution of artificial intelligence. Among these groundbreaking models, Llama stands as a testament to the rapid advancements in natural language processing. This book is a comprehensive exploration of Llama, delving deep into its architecture, training, optimization, and real-world applications.

Our aim is to empower developers, researchers, and enthusiasts with the knowledge and tools necessary to harness the full potential of Llama. From understanding the fundamental concepts to mastering advanced techniques, this book provides a structured approach to mastering this complex technology.

We have carefully curated the content to balance theoretical underpinnings with practical applications. The hands-on exercises and real-world examples offer opportunities to experiment and gain practical experience.

As the field of LLMs continues to evolve rapidly, this book serves as a solid foundation for understanding the current state of the art while providing a glimpse into future possibilities. We invite you to join us on this exciting journey as we explore the vast potential of Llama and its impact on the world.

Chapter 1: Introduction to Llama and Meta's Course

Chapter 1.1: Introduction

The Dawn of a New Era in Language Models

The advent of large language models (LLMs) has ushered in a new era of artificial intelligence, revolutionizing fields from natural language processing to computer vision. At the forefront of this revolution is Llama, a state-of-the-art LLM developed by Meta AI. This book delves deep into the intricacies of Llama, providing advanced developers with a comprehensive blueprint for mastering this powerful tool.

Llama represents a significant leap forward in natural language understanding and generation. Its ability to process and generate human-like text has opened up countless possibilities for applications, from content creation and translation to customer service and virtual assistants. Meta's decision to open-source Llama has democratized access to this technology, empowering a vast community of developers to explore its potential.

This book aims to equip you, the advanced developer, with the knowledge and skills necessary to harness the full power of Llama. By the end of this comprehensive guide, you will have a deep understanding of Llama's architecture, training methodologies, and optimization techniques. You will be able to confidently tackle complex challenges and develop cutting-edge applications that leverage Llama's capabilities.

Llama is a powerful language model developed by Meta AI. It stands for **Large Language Model Meta AI**. Essentially, it's a type of artificial intelligence designed to understand, interpret, and generate human-like text.

Llama is trained on massive amounts of text data, allowing it to learn patterns and relationships between words. This enables it to perform tasks such as:

Translation: Converting text from one language to another.

Summarization: Condensing long pieces of text into shorter versions.

Question answering: Providing informative answers to questions.

Text generation: Creating different kinds of creative text formats.

Llama is designed to be versatile and can be adapted to a wide range of applications.

The Significance of Llama in the AI Landscape

Llama's release has had a profound impact on the AI landscape. Its significance can be attributed to several key factors:

Open-sourcing: Unlike many other advanced LLMs, Llama was made open-source. This democratized access to powerful language models, fostering innovation and collaboration within the AI community.

Performance: Despite being open-source, Llama has demonstrated impressive performance across various benchmarks, competing with, and in some cases surpassing, closed-source models.

Research Catalyst: By making Llama accessible, Meta has accelerated research and development in the field of LLMs. This has led to numerous advancements and new applications.

Industry Impact: Llama's potential to be integrated into various industries is immense. From customer service chatbots to content generation, its applications are vast, promising to revolutionize how businesses operate.

Ethical Considerations: The open-source nature of Llama has sparked important conversations about the ethical implications of AI, encouraging responsible development and deployment of these powerful models.

By making Llama available to the public, Meta has significantly contributed to the advancement of AI and its potential to benefit society.

Meta's Role in Developing and Open-Sourcing Llama

Meta, formerly known as Facebook, has positioned itself as a pioneer in the realm of open-source AI. The development and subsequent open-sourcing of Llama is a testament to this commitment.

Massive Investment in Research: Meta has invested heavily in AI research, building a robust team of scientists and engineers dedicated to developing cutting-edge language models.

Training on Vast Datasets: To create a model as powerful as Llama, Meta leveraged its access to immense amounts of text data, allowing the model to learn complex patterns and nuances of language.

Open-Source Philosophy: In a departure from the trend of keeping advanced AI models proprietary, Meta made a strategic decision to open-source Llama. This move aimed to foster innovation, democratize access to AI, and accelerate the development of the field as a whole.

Driving AI Ecosystem: By open-sourcing Llama, Meta is actively shaping the AI ecosystem. It encourages collaboration, knowledge sharing, and the development of new applications built on top of the model.

Through these efforts, Meta has solidified its position as a leader in AI and demonstrated a strong commitment to open innovation.

The Purpose of This Book and Its Target Audience

Purpose:

This book aims to be the definitive guide for advanced developers seeking to master Llama, a cutting-edge language model developed by Meta AI. It provides a comprehensive exploration of Llama's architecture, training, optimization, and real-world applications. The goal is to equip readers with the knowledge and skills necessary to unlock the full potential of Llama and build innovative solutions.

Target Audience:

The primary target audience for this book is experienced developers with a strong foundation in machine learning and natural language processing. They should have a working knowledge of Python and be comfortable with complex technical concepts. Ideal readers include:

AI researchers

Data scientists

Machine learning engineers

Software developers with an interest in AI

Graduate students specializing in AI or related fields

By catering to this audience, the book will provide in-depth insights and practical guidance for those seeking to advance their Llama expertise.

Chapter 1.2: Key Concepts

Essential Terminology Related to Large Language Models (LLMs)

Before delving into the intricacies of Llama, it's crucial to grasp some fundamental terms associated with large language models:

Token: The basic unit of text processing in an LLM. It can be a word, part of a word, or a punctuation mark.

Embedding: A numerical representation of a word or phrase, capturing its semantic and syntactic meaning.

Transformer: The underlying architecture of many modern LLMs, including Llama, which excels at handling sequential data.

Attention Mechanism: A key component of transformers that allows the model to focus on different parts of the input sequence when making predictions.

Encoder-Decoder: The structure of many LLMs, where the encoder processes the input sequence, and the decoder generates the output sequence.

Core Components of an LLM Architecture

A typical LLM architecture comprises several key components:

Input Embedding Layer: Converts text into numerical representations (embeddings) suitable for the model.

Encoder Layers: Process the input sequence and generate contextual representations.

Decoder Layers: Generate the output sequence based on the encoder's output and previously generated tokens.

Output Layer: Converts the model's internal representations back into text.

How LLMs Learn and Generate Text

LLMs learn from massive amounts of text data through a process called training. During training, the model adjusts its parameters to minimize the difference between its predicted output and the actual text. This process is often referred to as "learning from examples."

When generating text, an LLM starts with an initial prompt or a few words and iteratively predicts the next word based on the context and its learned patterns. This process continues until the desired output length is reached or a stop token is encountered.

The Concept of Fine-Tuning and Its Importance

While pre-trained LLMs like Llama exhibit impressive capabilities, their performance can be further enhanced for specific tasks through a process called fine-tuning. Fine-tuning involves training the model on a smaller dataset tailored to the desired application. This allows the model to adapt its knowledge and generate more relevant and accurate outputs.

By understanding these core concepts, you'll be well-prepared to explore the intricacies of Llama and its applications.

Essential Terminology Related to Large Language Models (LLMs)

Core Terms

Token: The smallest unit of text processed by an LLM, which can be a word, part of a word, or a punctuation mark.

Embedding: A numerical representation of a word or phrase that captures its semantic and syntactic meaning.

Transformer: A neural network architecture that processes input data sequentially, paying attention to different parts of the input.

Attention Mechanism: A component of transformers that allows the model to focus on different parts of the input sequence when making predictions.

Encoder-Decoder: A common architecture for sequence-to-sequence models, where the encoder processes the input and the decoder generates the output.

Additional Terms

Pre-training: The initial phase of training an LLM on a massive amount of text data to learn general language patterns.

Fine-tuning: The process of adapting a pre-trained LLM to a specific task by training it on a smaller, task-specific dataset.

Overfitting: A phenomenon where a model performs exceptionally well on training data but poorly on new, unseen data.

Underfitting: A situation where a model is too simple to capture the underlying patterns in the data.

Hyperparameters: Parameters that control the training process of a model, such as learning rate, batch size, and number of epochs.

Evaluation Metrics

Perplexity: Measures how surprised a language model is by the text it encounters. Lower perplexity indicates better performance.

BLEU (Bilingual Evaluation Understudy): Commonly used to evaluate machine translation quality.

ROUGE (Recall-Oriented Understudy for Gisting Evaluation): Used to evaluate summarization tasks.

Understanding these terms is crucial for effectively working with and understanding large language models.

Core Components of an LLM Architecture

A typical LLM architecture consists of several key components working in tandem:

1. Input Embedding Layer

Converts text data into numerical representations (embeddings) that the model can understand.

Each word or token is mapped to a dense vector, capturing its semantic and syntactic meaning.

2. Encoder Layers

Process the input sequence and generate contextual representations.

Typically composed of multiple layers of self-attention and feed-forward neural networks.

Self-attention mechanism allows the model to weigh the importance of different parts of the input sequence.

3. Decoder Layers

Generate the output sequence one token at a time, conditioned on the encoder's output and previously generated tokens.

Similar architecture to the encoder but often includes additional components like attention over the encoder's output.

4. Output Layer

Converts the internal representations of the model back into text.

Maps the final hidden state of the decoder to a probability distribution over the vocabulary.

Visual Representation:

These core components work together to enable LLMs to process and generate human-like text. However, it's important to note that this is a simplified overview, and real-world LLMs often incorporate additional components and complexities.

How LLMs Learn and Generate Text

Learning Process (Training)

LLMs learn from massive amounts of text data through a process called *pre-training*. This involves feeding the model vast quantities of text and allowing it to learn patterns, relationships, and statistical regularities between words and sentences.

The training process typically involves:

Tokenization: Breaking down text into smaller units (tokens) for the model to process.

Embedding: Converting tokens into numerical representations (embeddings) that capture their meaning.

Model Architecture: Using a neural network architecture, such as a transformer, to process the text data.

Backpropagation: Adjusting the model's parameters to minimize the difference between its predicted output and the actual text.

Text Generation Process

Once trained, an LLM can generate text by:

Providing a prompt: This can be a single word, a sentence, or even a longer piece of text.

Generating the first token: The model predicts the most likely next token based on the prompt and its learned patterns.

Iterative generation: The model continues to generate subsequent tokens, using the previously generated text as a context.

Decoding: The model converts the generated token IDs back into text.

Key techniques for text generation:

Greedy search: Selecting the most probable token at each step.

Beam search: Considering multiple candidate sequences at each step and selecting the best overall sequence.

Sampling: Randomly selecting a token based on its probability distribution.

It's important to note that the quality of generated text depends on various factors, including the size and quality of the training data, the model architecture, and the chosen generation method.

The Concept of Fine-Tuning and Its Importance

Fine-tuning is the process of adapting a pre-trained language model to a specific task or domain by training it on a smaller, task-specific dataset. It's essentially taking a model that has learned general language patterns and specializing it for a particular purpose.

Importance of Fine-Tuning

Improved Performance: Fine-tuning allows a model to better understand the nuances of a specific task, leading to improved performance compared to using a pre-trained model directly.

Efficiency: Training a model from scratch on a large dataset is computationally expensive and time-consuming. Fine-tuning leverages the knowledge already acquired by the pre-trained model, significantly reducing training time and resources.

Customization: By fine-tuning on task-specific data, models can be tailored to specific domains or user preferences, resulting in more relevant and accurate outputs.

Data Efficiency: Fine-tuning often requires less training data compared to training a model from scratch, making it more feasible for tasks with limited available data.

Example: A pre-trained LLM might be able to generate general text, but fine-tuning it on a dataset of medical articles would allow it to generate text specifically related to medical topics, such as patient summaries or drug information.

Chapter 1.3: Hands-on Exercises

Note: These exercises assume basic familiarity with Python and a Python environment (like Anaconda or Jupyter Notebook). You might need to install additional libraries like `transformers` and `torch`.

Exercise 1.1: Setting Up the Environment

Install necessary libraries:

Bash

```
pip install transformers torch
```

Import required libraries:

Python

```python
import torch

from transformers import AutoModelForCausalLM,
AutoTokenizer
```

Exercise 1.2: Loading a Pre-trained Llama Model

Load a pre-trained Llama model and its tokenizer:

Python

```python
model_name = "meta-llama/llama-7b"    # Replace
with desired model size

tokenizer                              =
AutoTokenizer.from_pretrained(model_name)

model                                  =
AutoModelForCausalLM.from_pretrained(model_name)
```

Exercise 1.3: Generating Text

Generate text using the loaded model:

Python

```python
prompt = "Hello, world!"

input_ids = tokenizer(prompt, return_tensors="pt").input_ids


# Generate text

output = model.generate(input_ids, max_length=50, do_sample=True)


# Decode the output

generated_text = tokenizer.decode(output[0], skip_special_tokens=True)

print(generated_text)
```

Exercise 1.4: Experimenting with Different Parameters

Try different values for `max_length`, `do_sample`, `temperature`, and `top_p` to observe the effects on the generated text.

Experiment with different prompts to see how the model responds.

Exercise 1.5: Evaluating Model Performance

While not exhaustive, try to qualitatively assess the generated text.

Consider using basic metrics like perplexity if you have a reference text.

Additional Exercises (Optional):

Experiment with different Llama model sizes (e.g., 7B, 13B).

Try fine-tuning a smaller Llama model on a specific task (e.g., text summarization, question answering).

Explore techniques for improving generation quality, such as beam search or nucleus sampling.

Remember:

Always respect ethical guidelines when working with language models.

Be mindful of computational resources, especially for larger models.

Experimentation is key to understanding the capabilities and limitations of LLMs.

By completing these exercises, you'll gain hands-on experience with Llama and develop a foundation for exploring more advanced topics in the following chapters.

Setting Up the Environment for Llama Development

Hardware Requirements

Before we dive into the software setup, it's essential to consider your hardware. Training and fine-tuning large language models like Llama are computationally intensive. You'll need a machine with:

Powerful GPU: NVIDIA GPUs with ample VRAM are recommended.

Sufficient RAM: At least 32GB, but more is preferable.

Large Storage: To accommodate the model weights and training data.

If you don't have access to such hardware, consider cloud-based solutions like Google Colab, AWS, or GCP.

Software Prerequisites

Python Environment:

Install Python (version 3.7 or later).

Create a virtual environment to isolate project dependencies:

Bash

```
python -m venv llama_env

source llama_env/bin/activate   # On Linux/macOS

llama_env\Scripts\activate   # On Windows
```

Essential Libraries:

Install required libraries using pip:

Bash

```bash
pip install transformers torch datasets
```

Other libraries might be needed depending on your specific tasks (e.g., `numpy`, `pandas`).

Obtaining the Llama Model

Meta's Official Channels: Check Meta's official channels for announcements about model availability and licensing terms.

Hugging Face: Many pre-trained Llama models are available on Hugging Face. You can download them using the `transformers` library:

Python

```python
from transformers import AutoModelForCausalLM, AutoTokenizer
```

```
model_name = "meta-llama/llama-7b"    # Replace
with desired model

tokenizer                                     =
AutoTokenizer.from_pretrained(model_name)

model                                         =
AutoModelForCausalLM.from_pretrained(model_name)
```

Additional Considerations

GPU Acceleration: Ensure your Python environment and libraries are configured to utilize your GPU.

Computational Resources: Training large language models can be computationally expensive. Consider using cloud-based platforms or distributed training if necessary.

Data Preparation: If you plan to fine-tune the model, you'll need to prepare your dataset accordingly. This might involve cleaning, preprocessing, and formatting the data.

By following these steps, you'll establish a solid foundation for your Llama development projects.

Basic Interactions with the Llama Model

Once you've set up your environment and loaded a Llama model, you can start interacting with it.

Generating Text

The most basic interaction is generating text based on a given prompt.

Python

```python
import torch

from transformers import AutoModelForCausalLM,
AutoTokenizer


model_name = "meta-llama/llama-7b"    # Replace
with desired model size

tokenizer                                          =
AutoTokenizer.from_pretrained(model_name)

model                                              =
AutoModelForCausalLM.from_pretrained(model_name)


prompt = "What is the capital of France?"

input_ids              =             tokenizer(prompt,
return_tensors="pt").input_ids


# Generate text

output = model.generate(input_ids, max_length=30,
do_sample=True)
```

```
# Decode the output

generated_text    =    tokenizer.decode(output[0],
skip_special_tokens=True)

print(generated_text)
```

Controlling Generation Behavior

You can control the generated text by adjusting parameters:

`max_length`: Sets the maximum length of the generated text.

`do_sample`: If True, uses sampling to generate text, otherwise uses greedy decoding.

`temperature`: Controls the randomness of the generated text. Higher temperature leads to more diverse outputs.

`top_p`: Sets a cumulative probability for token selection.

Handling Different Prompts

You can experiment with different prompts to explore the model's capabilities:

Factual questions: "Who is the president of the United States?"

Open-ended questions: "What is the meaning of life?"

Creative writing prompts: "Write a poem about a robot exploring Mars."

Translation: "Translate 'Hello, how are you?' into Spanish."

Experimentation

The best way to understand a model is to experiment with it. Try different prompts, parameters, and tasks to discover its strengths and limitations.

Exploring Llama's Capabilities Through Simple Examples

Let's dive deeper into Llama's abilities by experimenting with different prompts and tasks.

Text Summarization

Python

```python
prompt = "The quick brown fox jumps over the lazy
dog. This is a simple sentence to test text
summarization."
```

Question Answering

Python

```python
prompt = "Who wrote the play Hamlet?"
```

Translation

Python

```python
prompt = "Translate 'Hello, how are you?' into Spanish."
```

Text Generation

Python

```python
prompt = "Write a short story about a robot who wants to be a chef."
```

Code Generation (Basic)

Python

```python
prompt = "Write a Python function to calculate factorial of a number."
```

Story Telling

Python

```python
prompt = "Once upon a time..."
```

Note: For more complex tasks like code generation or creative writing, you might need to experiment with different prompts, parameters, and potentially fine-tune the model.

Chapter 2: Deep Dive into Llama Architecture

Chapter 2.1: Introduction

While we've explored Llama's capabilities at a surface level, a deeper understanding of its architecture is crucial for maximizing its potential. This chapter delves into the technical underpinnings of Llama, providing insights into how it processes information and generates text.

Why is understanding Llama's architecture important?

Optimizing performance: By understanding the internal workings, you can fine-tune parameters and techniques to improve model performance on specific tasks.

Troubleshooting issues: When encountering problems, knowledge of the architecture can help identify potential causes and solutions.

Developing custom models: A deep understanding of Llama can serve as a foundation for building your own language models.

Pushing the boundaries: Exploring the architecture can inspire new ideas for improving language models and their applications.

In the following sections, we will dissect Llama's architecture, exploring its core components and how they interact to produce remarkable results.

Chapter 2.2: Key Concepts

Transformer Architecture

Llama, like many modern language models, is built upon the transformer architecture. This architecture has revolutionized natural language processing due to its effectiveness in handling sequential data.

Key components of the transformer:

Self-attention: This mechanism allows the model to weigh the importance of different parts of the input sequence when processing a specific part. It enables the model to capture long-range dependencies.

Encoder-Decoder Structure: While the original transformer was designed for machine translation, Llama uses an encoder-only architecture. The encoder processes the input sequence, and the output is used for various downstream tasks.

Positional Encoding: Since transformers process input as a sequence of embeddings, positional information is lost. Positional encoding adds information about the position of each token in the sequence.

Model Size and Parameters

The size of a language model is determined by the number of parameters. A larger model typically has more capacity to learn complex patterns and generate higher-quality text. However, it also requires more computational resources for training and inference.

Activation Functions

Activation functions introduce non-linearity into the neural network, enabling it to learn complex patterns. Common activation functions used in language models include:

ReLU (Rectified Linear Unit): Introduces non-linearity while being computationally efficient.

GELU (Gaussian Error Linear Unit): A smooth approximation of ReLU, often used in transformer-based models.

Normalization Techniques

Normalization techniques help stabilize training and improve model performance. Common methods include:

Layer Normalization: Normalizes the activations of each layer independently.

Batch Normalization: Normalizes activations across a batch of training examples.

Loss Function

The loss function measures the difference between the model's predicted output and the actual target. Common loss functions for language models include:

Cross-entropy loss: Measures the difference between the predicted probability distribution and the true distribution of the target token.

By understanding these key concepts, we lay the groundwork for a deeper exploration of Llama's architecture in the following sections.

Chapter 2.3: Hands-on Exercises

While theoretical understanding is crucial, practical experimentation solidifies knowledge. Let's explore some hands-on exercises to reinforce the concepts discussed in this chapter.

Exercise 1: Visualizing the Attention Mechanism

Objective: Gain an intuitive understanding of how the attention mechanism works.

Steps:

Use a visualization library like Matplotlib or Seaborn to plot attention weights.

Choose a short input sequence and visualize the attention matrix.

Analyze the patterns in the attention weights to understand how the model focuses on different parts of the input.

Exercise 2: Experimenting with Model Sizes

Objective: Observe the impact of model size on performance.

Steps:

Train or fine-tune Llama models with different numbers of parameters.

Evaluate the models on a benchmark dataset.

Analyze the trade-offs between model size, performance, and computational resources.

Exercise 3: Analyzing the Impact of Hyperparameters

Objective: Understand how hyperparameters influence model training and performance.

Steps:

Experiment with different hyperparameter values (learning rate, batch size, number of epochs).

Train multiple models with varying hyperparameters.

Compare the performance of these models to identify optimal hyperparameter settings.

Note: These exercises require access to computational resources and potentially large datasets. Cloud-based platforms or high-performance computing clusters can be helpful for larger experiments.

By completing these exercises, you'll develop a deeper intuition for Llama's architecture and gain practical experience in working with language models.

Chapter 3: Mastering Llama Training Fundamentals

Chapter 3.1: Introduction

Building upon our understanding of Llama's architecture, we now shift our focus to the critical process of training these complex models. Effective training is the cornerstone of creating powerful and versatile language models. This chapter will lay the groundwork for mastering the art of training Llama.

Training a language model is a multifaceted process involving data preparation, model architecture, optimization algorithms, and evaluation. Understanding these components is essential for achieving optimal performance.

In the following sections, we will delve into the key aspects of Llama training, providing insights and practical guidance to help you build exceptional models.

Chapter 3.2: Key Concepts

Data Preparation

High-quality data is the cornerstone of effective model training. The process involves several key steps:

Data Collection: Gathering relevant and diverse text data from various sources.

Cleaning: Removing noise, inconsistencies, and errors from the data.

Preprocessing: Tokenization, lowercasing, removing stop words, and handling out-of-vocabulary words.

Data Formatting: Structuring data into a suitable format for model training (e.g., text files, CSV).

Training Objectives

Clearly defined training objectives guide the model's learning process. Common objectives include:

Language Modeling: Predicting the next word in a sequence.

Masked Language Modeling: Predicting masked words within a text sequence.

Next Sentence Prediction: Predicting whether two sentences follow each other.

Causal Language Modeling: Generating text sequentially, one token at a time.

Optimization Algorithms

Optimization algorithms adjust model parameters to minimize the loss function. Key methods include:

Gradient Descent: Iteratively updating parameters in the direction of steepest descent.

Adam: Adaptive Moment Estimation, combining the advantages of AdaGrad and RMSprop.

Other Optimizers: Exploring options like Adagrad, RMSprop, and variations of Adam.

Regularization

Regularization techniques help prevent overfitting and improve generalization:

L1/L2 Regularization: Adding penalties to the loss function based on the magnitude of model parameters.

Dropout: Randomly dropping units during training to reduce reliance on specific neurons.

Early Stopping: Stopping training when validation performance starts to degrade.

Learning Rate Scheduling

Adjusting the learning rate during training can accelerate convergence and improve performance:

Step Decay: Reducing the learning rate at specific intervals.

Exponential Decay: Gradually decreasing the learning rate over time.

Learning Rate Warmup: Increasing the learning rate initially before decaying.

By understanding these key concepts, you'll be well-equipped to design effective training strategies for Llama models.

Chapter 3.3: Hands-on Exercises

Exercise 1: Data Cleaning and Preprocessing

Objective: Understand the impact of data quality on model performance.

Steps:

Collect a raw text dataset (e.g., news articles, books).

Implement functions to clean the text (remove stop words, punctuation, special characters).

Experiment with different tokenization techniques (word-level, subword-level).

Train a small-scale model on both cleaned and uncleaned data to compare results.

Exercise 2: Hyperparameter Tuning

Objective: Find optimal hyperparameters for Llama training.

Steps:

Define a search space for hyperparameters (learning rate, batch size, number of epochs, etc.).

Use a hyperparameter optimization library (e.g., Optuna, Ray Tune) or grid search.

Train multiple models with different hyperparameter combinations.

Evaluate model performance using appropriate metrics.

Exercise 3: Experimenting with Different Optimizers

Objective: Compare the performance of different optimization algorithms.

Steps:

Train multiple models using different optimizers (Adam, AdamW, SGD, etc.).

Monitor training loss and validation metrics.

Analyze the convergence speed and final performance of each optimizer.

Exercise 4: Implementing Regularization Techniques

Objective: Understand the impact of regularization on model performance.

Steps:

Train models with different regularization strengths (L1, L2, dropout).

Evaluate models on a validation set to assess overfitting.

Analyze the effect of regularization on model complexity and generalization.

Additional Exercises:

Experiment with different learning rate schedules.

Implement early stopping to prevent overfitting.

Try data augmentation techniques to improve model robustness.

Note: These exercises require computational resources and may take time to complete. Consider using cloud-based platforms or GPU acceleration for larger-scale experiments.

By conducting these hands-on exercises, you'll gain practical experience in training Llama models and develop a deeper understanding of the factors influencing model performance.

Chapter 4: Advanced Techniques for Fine-Tuning Llama Models

Chapter 4.1: Introduction

While we've established a strong foundation in training foundational language models, the true power of LLMs lies in their adaptability to specific tasks. **Fine-tuning** is the process of adapting a pre-trained model to excel in a particular domain or application.

This chapter will delve into advanced techniques to optimize Llama for specific use cases. We'll explore how to tailor the model to perform exceptionally well on tasks ranging from sentiment analysis to question answering, while maintaining the core strengths of the pre-trained model.

By understanding these techniques, you'll be able to create highly specialized and effective Llama models for a wide range of applications.

Chapter 4.2: Key Concepts

Fine-Tuning Strategies

Fine-tuning involves adapting a pre-trained model to a specific task. Several strategies exist:

Full Fine-Tuning: Adjusting all model parameters on the new task. This can be effective but computationally expensive.

Adapter Tuning: Introducing additional trainable parameters (adapters) to the pre-trained model, leaving the core model weights frozen. This approach is often more efficient.

Prompt Tuning: Modifying the input prompt to guide the model's output without changing model parameters. This can be effective for certain tasks but might require careful prompt engineering.

Handling Imbalanced Datasets

Many real-world datasets exhibit class imbalance, where one class has significantly more examples than others. Techniques to address this include:

Oversampling: Increasing the number of instances in the minority class through techniques like duplication or synthetic data generation.

Undersampling: Reducing the number of instances in the majority class.

Class Weighting: Assigning different weights to different classes during training to balance their impact.

Transfer Learning

Leveraging knowledge from a pre-trained model to accelerate learning on a new task is known as transfer learning. This technique can significantly improve performance, especially with limited data.

Knowledge Distillation

Transferring knowledge from a large, complex teacher model to a smaller, faster student model is called knowledge distillation. This technique can create more efficient models while preserving much of the original model's performance.

Evaluation Metrics

Beyond accuracy, other metrics are crucial for evaluating fine-tuned models:

Precision: The proportion of positive predictions that are truly positive.

Recall: The proportion of actual positives that are correctly identified.

F1-score: The harmonic mean of precision and recall.

AUC-ROC: Area under the Receiver Operating Characteristic curve, used for classification tasks.

Understanding these concepts will equip you to effectively fine-tune Llama models for various applications.

Chapter 4.3: Hands-on Exercises

Exercise 1: Experiment with Different Fine-Tuning Strategies

Objective: Compare the performance of full fine-tuning, adapter tuning, and prompt tuning on a text classification task.

Steps:

Choose a suitable dataset (e.g., IMDB sentiment analysis).

Implement each fine-tuning strategy.

Evaluate models based on accuracy, precision, recall, and F1-score.

Analyze the trade-offs between performance and computational efficiency.

Exercise 2: Handling Imbalanced Datasets

Objective: Improve model performance on imbalanced datasets.

Steps:

Create an imbalanced dataset (e.g., artificially imbalance a sentiment analysis dataset).

Implement oversampling, undersampling, and class weighting techniques.

Evaluate model performance using appropriate metrics.

Analyze the impact of different imbalance handling methods.

Exercise 3: Implement Transfer Learning

Objective: Leverage knowledge from a pre-trained model for a new task.

Steps:

Choose a source task and a target task (e.g., language modeling as the source, text summarization as the target).

Fine-tune the pre-trained model on the target task.

Compare the performance of the fine-tuned model to a model trained from scratch.

Exercise 4: Explore Knowledge Distillation

Objective: Transfer knowledge from a large teacher model to a smaller student model.

Steps:

Train a large teacher model on a substantial dataset.

Train a smaller student model using the teacher model's outputs as soft targets.

Evaluate the student model's performance compared to the teacher model.

Additional Exercises:

Experiment with different hyperparameters for fine-tuning.

Explore the use of domain-specific datasets for fine-tuning.

Investigate techniques for handling long-tail distributions in imbalanced datasets.

By conducting these hands-on exercises, you will gain practical experience in fine-tuning Llama models and develop a deeper understanding of the techniques discussed in this chapter.

Chapter 5: Unlocking Llama's Optimization Potential

Chapter 5.1: Introduction

While we've successfully explored the foundations of training and fine-tuning Llama models, our journey to optimize their performance is far from over. This chapter delves into the critical area of **model optimization**.

As the computational demands of large language models continue to grow, there's a pressing need to balance performance with efficiency. This chapter will explore strategies to streamline these models without compromising their capabilities.

We'll discuss techniques to reduce model size, accelerate inference, and deploy models effectively in various environments. By the end of this chapter, you'll be equipped to optimize Llama models for real-world applications, ensuring they deliver exceptional performance while meeting resource constraints.

Let's dive into the core concepts of model optimization.

Chapter 5.2: Key Concepts

Quantization

Quantization involves reducing the precision of model weights and activations. This leads to smaller model sizes and faster inference times. There are several quantization techniques, including:

Post-training quantization: Applying quantization without retraining the model.

Quantization-aware training: Training the model with quantization in mind to improve accuracy.

Model Compression

Model compression techniques aim to reduce the size of the model without significant performance degradation. Common methods include:

Pruning: Removing unnecessary weights or neurons from the model.

Weight Sharing: Sharing weights among different neurons to reduce the number of parameters.

Low-Rank Approximation: Approximating the weight matrix with a lower-rank matrix.

Hardware Acceleration

Leveraging specialized hardware can significantly accelerate model inference. Key considerations include:

GPU Acceleration: Utilizing GPUs for parallel computations.

TPU Acceleration: Employing Tensor Processing Units designed for machine learning workloads.

Hardware-Specific Optimizations: Tailoring the model and code for specific hardware architectures.

Model Deployment

Deploying a model in a production environment requires careful consideration:

Cloud-Based Platforms: Utilizing cloud services for model hosting and serving.

Edge Devices: Deploying models on devices with limited computational resources.

Model Serving Frameworks: Using frameworks like TensorFlow Serving or TorchServe for efficient deployment.

Emerging Trends

The field of model optimization is rapidly evolving:

Neural Architecture Search (NAS): Automatically finding optimal model architectures.

Quantization-Aware Training (QAT): Improving quantization accuracy through training.

Sparse Neural Networks: Exploiting sparsity in model weights for efficiency.

Hybrid Approaches: Combining multiple optimization techniques for maximum benefit.

By understanding these concepts, you can effectively optimize Llama models for various deployment scenarios.

Chapter 5.3: Hands-on Exercises

Exercise 1: Experiment with Quantization

Objective: Reduce model size while preserving performance.

Steps:

Quantize a pre-trained Llama model to lower precision (e.g., INT8).

Evaluate the quantized model's performance on a benchmark dataset.

Compare model size, inference speed, and accuracy before and after quantization.

Exercise 2: Implement Model Pruning

Objective: Reduce model complexity while maintaining performance.

Steps:

Identify unimportant weights or neurons in the Llama model.

Prune the model by removing these weights or neurons.

Retrain the pruned model to recover performance.

Evaluate the pruned model's size, speed, and accuracy.

Exercise 3: Optimize for Different Hardware

Objective: Accelerate model inference on different hardware platforms.

Steps:

Run inference on a CPU, GPU, and TPU (if available).

Profile the model's performance on each platform.

Identify performance bottlenecks and optimize code accordingly.

Compare inference speed and resource utilization across platforms.

Exercise 4: Explore Model Deployment Options

Objective: Deploy a Llama model for serving predictions.
Steps:

Choose a cloud platform (e.g., AWS, GCP, Azure).

Create a containerized deployment of the Llama model.

Implement a REST API for serving predictions.

Test the deployed model with different input requests.

Additional Exercises:

Experiment with different quantization levels and techniques.

Combine pruning with quantization for further model compression.

Explore hardware-specific optimizations (e.g., GPU kernels, tensor cores).

Evaluate the trade-offs between model size, speed, and accuracy for different deployment scenarios.

By completing these exercises, you will gain practical experience in optimizing Llama models for various constraints and environments.

Chapter 6: Real-World Applications of Advanced Llama Techniques

Chapter 6.1: Introduction

While the preceding chapters have focused on the technical intricacies of building and optimizing Llama models, this chapter shifts our attention to the practical applications of these powerful tools. We'll explore how to bridge the gap between theoretical knowledge and real-world problem-solving.

The potential applications of Llama are vast and diverse, spanning across various industries and domains. By understanding how to tailor these models to specific use cases, we can unlock their full potential and create innovative solutions.

In the following sections, we'll delve into real-world examples, industry-specific applications, and the ethical considerations that accompany the deployment of such powerful technology.

Let's explore the exciting world of Llama applications!

Chapter 6.2: Key Concepts

Industry-Specific Adaptations

To maximize Llama's potential, it's essential to tailor the model to specific industry needs. This involves:

Domain-specific data: Training or fine-tuning Llama on industry-relevant data.

Custom vocabularies: Incorporating domain-specific terms into the model's vocabulary.

Performance metrics: Defining industry-specific evaluation metrics.

Hybrid Models

Combining Llama with other AI techniques can create powerful hybrid models. For example:

Llama + Computer Vision: Analyzing visual content and generating text descriptions.

Llama + Speech Recognition: Converting spoken language to text for further processing.

User Experience Design

Creating intuitive interfaces for interacting with Llama-powered applications is crucial for user adoption. Key considerations include:

Natural language understanding: Enabling users to interact with the model using natural language.

Contextual awareness: Understanding user intent and providing relevant responses.

Personalization: Tailoring the user experience based on individual preferences.

Ethical Considerations

Developing and deploying Llama models responsibly is essential. Key ethical considerations include:

Bias mitigation: Identifying and addressing biases in training data and model outputs.

Privacy protection: Ensuring user data is handled securely and responsibly.

Transparency: Communicating the limitations and potential biases of the model.

Accountability: Establishing clear guidelines for model development and deployment.

By understanding these key concepts, you can build Llama-powered applications that are both effective and responsible.

Would you like to delve deeper into a specific concept or proceed to the hands-on exercises?

Chapter 6.3: Hands-on Exercises

Exercise 1: Build a Chatbot

Objective: Create a chatbot for a specific domain (e.g., customer support, e-commerce).

Steps:

Define the chatbot's personality and tone.

Collect and preprocess a dataset of relevant conversations.

Fine-tune a Llama model on the dataset.

Implement a chatbot interface using a framework like Rasa or Dialogflow.

Evaluate the chatbot's performance based on user satisfaction metrics.

Exercise 2: Create a Content Generator

Objective: Develop a content generation tool for a specific niche (e.g., blog posts, social media content).

Steps:

Define content formats and styles.

Collect and preprocess a dataset of relevant content.

Fine-tune a Llama model for text generation.

Create a user interface for generating content.

Evaluate the quality and relevance of generated content.

Exercise 3: Explore Sentiment Analysis

Objective: Build a sentiment analysis tool for social media or customer reviews.

Steps:

Collect and preprocess a labeled dataset of text with sentiment annotations.

Fine-tune a Llama model for sentiment classification.

Evaluate the model's performance using metrics like accuracy, precision, recall, and F1-score.

Explore techniques for handling sarcasm and irony.

Exercise 4: Develop a Question Answering System

Objective: Create a question answering system for a specific knowledge base.

Steps:

Prepare a dataset of questions and answers.

Fine-tune a Llama model for question answering.

Evaluate the system's performance using metrics like accuracy and F1-score.

Explore techniques for handling complex questions and providing informative answers.

Note: For each exercise, consider ethical implications and biases. Iterate on your models based on user feedback and performance evaluation.

By engaging in these hands-on projects, you'll gain practical experience in applying Llama to real-world problems and develop a deeper understanding of its capabilities and limitations.

Chapter 7: Debugging and Troubleshooting Common Llama Issues

Chapter 7.1: Introduction

Building and training complex models like Llama is an iterative process fraught with challenges. While the previous chapters have focused on the ideal development path, the reality often involves unexpected hurdles. This chapter shifts our focus to the inevitable: troubleshooting and debugging.

From understanding error messages to optimizing performance, this chapter will equip you with the tools and strategies to overcome common obstacles and ensure the smooth development of your Llama models.

Let's dive into the world of troubleshooting and debugging.

Chapter 7.2: Key Concepts

Error Handling

Understanding and effectively handling errors is crucial for successful model development. Key concepts include:

Common error types: Syntax errors, runtime errors, and logical errors.

Error messages: Interpreting error messages to identify the root cause.

Debugging techniques: Using print statements, debuggers, and logging to isolate issues.

Debugging Tools

Leveraging debugging tools can significantly accelerate the troubleshooting process:

Python debuggers: Using tools like pdb or IDE-integrated debuggers to step through code execution.

Profilers: Identifying performance bottlenecks and optimizing code.

Visualization tools: Using tools to visualize model behavior and data.

Performance Bottlenecks

Optimizing model performance often involves identifying and addressing bottlenecks:

Hardware limitations: Recognizing constraints imposed by CPU, GPU, or memory.

Algorithmic inefficiencies: Identifying areas for optimization in code and model architecture.

Data-related issues: Addressing data quality and preprocessing problems.

Model Evaluation Metrics

Selecting appropriate metrics is essential for assessing model performance and identifying areas for improvement:

Relevance of metrics: Choosing metrics that align with the model's goals.

Multiple metrics: Using a combination of metrics for a comprehensive evaluation.

Baseline comparison: Comparing model performance to established benchmarks.

Iterative Development

A key to successful model development is adopting an iterative approach:

Experimentation: Trying different approaches and hyperparameters.

Feedback loop: Continuously evaluating and refining the model.

Version control: Tracking changes and enabling rollback.

By mastering these key concepts, you'll be well-equipped to tackle common challenges and optimize your Llama models.

Chapter 7.3: Hands-on Exercises

Exercise 1: Reproducing Errors

Create a script with intentional errors (syntax, runtime, logical).

Implement error handling mechanisms to catch and handle these errors.

Analyze the error messages to understand their causes.

Exercise 2: Using a Debugger

Set up a breakpoint in your code using a debugger (e.g., pdb, PyCharm debugger).

Step through the code line by line to inspect variables and identify issues.

Use conditional breakpoints to focus on specific code sections.

Exercise 3: Profiling Model Performance

Use a profiler (e.g., cProfile, line_profiler) to identify performance bottlenecks in your code.

Optimize code sections with high execution time.

Compare performance before and after optimization.

Exercise 4: Experimenting with Evaluation Metrics

Evaluate a model using different metrics (accuracy, precision, recall, F1-score, etc.).

Analyze the strengths and weaknesses of the model based on the metrics.

Identify areas for improvement by focusing on specific metrics.

Exercise 5: Iterative Model Improvement

Train a baseline model and evaluate its performance.

Modify hyperparameters, architecture, or data preprocessing.

Retrain the model and evaluate the new performance.

Iterate this process until satisfactory results are achieved.

By completing these exercises, you'll develop a strong foundation in debugging and troubleshooting Llama models, leading to more efficient and effective development cycles.

Chapter 8: Pushing the Boundaries: Exploring Cutting-Edge Llama Research

Chapter 8.1: Introduction

The field of large language models is in a state of constant evolution. While we've covered the foundational aspects and advanced techniques, the true frontier of LLM development lies in exploring the cutting edge. This chapter ventures into the uncharted territory of Llama research, examining the latest breakthroughs and potential future directions.

We'll delve into emerging trends, innovative applications, and the ethical implications of pushing the boundaries of language models. By understanding the forefront of LLM research, you'll be equipped to contribute to this rapidly evolving field and develop groundbreaking applications.

Let's embark on this exploration of the future of Llama.

Chapter 8.2: Key Concepts

Reinforcement Learning from Human Feedback (RLHF)

RLHF is a technique that aligns language models with human preferences. By providing human feedback on model outputs, the model can be trained to generate text that is more consistent with human values and expectations.

In-Context Learning

In-context learning allows models to adapt to new tasks without explicit retraining. By providing a few examples of the desired output format, the model can generate similar outputs for unseen data.

Multimodal Models

Multimodal models can process and generate multiple types of data, such as text, images, and audio. This capability enables more complex and interactive applications.

Interpretability and Explainability

Understanding how LLMs arrive at their decisions is crucial for building trust and identifying potential biases. Interpretability and explainability techniques aim to shed light on the model's internal workings.

Ethical Challenges

As LLMs become more powerful, addressing ethical concerns becomes increasingly important. This includes:

Bias: Identifying and mitigating biases in training data and model outputs.

Misinformation: Preventing the generation of harmful or misleading content.

Privacy: Protecting user data and preventing sensitive information leakage.

Job displacement: Assessing the potential impact of LLMs on the workforce.

These concepts represent the forefront of LLM research and development. By understanding these areas, you can stay updated on the latest advancements and contribute to the field.

Chapter 8.3: Hands-on Exercises (Exploratory)

Note: These exercises are exploratory in nature and may require significant computational resources and expertise.

Exercise 1: Experiment with RLHF

Objective: Build a basic RLHF setup for a simple task like sentiment analysis.

Steps:

Collect a dataset of text examples with human-provided ratings.

Train a reward model to predict human preferences.

Implement a reinforcement learning algorithm to fine-tune the language model.

Evaluate the model's performance before and after RLHF.

Exercise 2: Explore In-Context Learning

Objective: Test the in-context learning capabilities of Llama on different tasks.

Steps:

Choose various tasks (text summarization, question answering, translation).

Provide a few examples of the desired output format without explicit training.

Evaluate the model's ability to generate accurate outputs.

Exercise 3: Investigate Multimodal Applications

Objective: Combine text with other modalities (e.g., image, audio) for a creative project.

Steps:

Choose a multimodal task (e.g., image captioning, video description).

Explore existing multimodal models or build a custom model.

Evaluate the model's performance and identify potential challenges.

Exercise 4: Analyze Model Bias

Objective: Identify potential biases in a Llama model.

Steps:

Choose a specific bias to investigate (e.g., gender, race).

Analyze the model's outputs on different datasets.

Use bias detection tools or techniques.

Propose potential mitigation strategies.

Remember: These exercises are exploratory and may require significant computational resources and expertise. It's essential to approach these experiments with a focus on learning and experimentation rather than immediate results.

Chapter 9: Best Practices for Integrating Llama into Your Projects

Chapter 9.1: Introduction

While we've delved deep into the technical intricacies of building and optimizing Llama models, the true value lies in their successful integration into real-world applications. This chapter shifts our focus from the theoretical to the practical, exploring the best practices for incorporating Llama into your projects.

Successfully integrating a large language model requires careful planning, execution, and ongoing management. We'll discuss essential considerations for ensuring a smooth integration process and maximizing the value of your Llama model.

Let's explore the key steps to successfully integrating Llama into your projects.

Chapter 9.2: Key Concepts

Project Planning

Successful Llama integration starts with thorough project planning:

Define project goals: Clearly outline the desired outcomes and objectives.

Identify target users: Understand the needs and expectations of end-users.

Assess resource requirements: Determine the necessary computational resources, data, and personnel.

Risk assessment: Identify potential challenges and develop mitigation strategies.

Model Selection

Choosing the right Llama model is crucial for project success:

Evaluate model capabilities: Assess the model's strengths and weaknesses.

Consider computational constraints: Balance model size with available resources.

Experiment with different models: Test multiple models to find the best fit.

Data Integration

Integrating Llama with existing data sources is often necessary:

Data preprocessing: Prepare data for compatibility with the model.

Data enrichment: Combine Llama-generated content with other data sources.

Data privacy: Ensure compliance with data protection regulations.

API Development

Creating a user-friendly interface is essential for interacting with the Llama model:

REST API: Develop a RESTful API for external applications.

Language-specific bindings: Provide libraries for different programming languages.

Error handling: Implement robust error handling mechanisms.

Performance Optimization

Ensuring optimal Llama performance is crucial for user satisfaction:

Hardware acceleration: Utilize GPUs or TPUs for faster inference.

Model optimization: Apply techniques like quantization or pruning.

Batching: Process multiple requests simultaneously.

Monitoring and Evaluation

Continuous monitoring and evaluation are essential for improvement:

Key performance indicators (KPIs): Define metrics to measure model performance.

User feedback: Collect user input to refine the model.

A/B testing: Experiment with different model configurations.

By understanding these key concepts, you can effectively plan and execute Llama integration projects.

Chapter 9.3: Hands-on Exercises

Exercise 1: Define a Project Scope

Objective: Clearly outline a potential project using Llama.
Steps:

Identify a specific problem or opportunity.

Define project goals and objectives.

Create a user persona to understand target users.

Outline project requirements and deliverables.

Exercise 2: Select and Integrate a Llama Model

Objective: Choose and integrate a Llama model into a sample application.
Steps:

Select a Llama model based on project requirements.

Integrate the model into a Python or other programming environment.

Experiment with different prompts and inputs.

Evaluate model performance in the context of the application.

Exercise 3: Develop a REST API

Objective: Create a RESTful API to expose Llama's capabilities.

Steps:

Choose a framework (e.g., Flask, FastAPI).

Define API endpoints and request/response formats.

Implement API logic to interact with the Llama model.

Test the API using tools like Postman or curl.

Exercise 4: Implement Performance Monitoring

Objective: Track model performance and identify areas for improvement.

Steps:

Define key performance indicators (KPIs).

Implement monitoring tools or libraries.

Collect and analyze performance data.

Identify bottlenecks and optimization opportunities.

Exercise 5: Iterate and Improve

Objective: Continuously refine the model and application based on feedback.

Steps:

Collect user feedback and analyze performance metrics.

Identify areas for improvement.

Experiment with different model configurations or data.

Redeploy the model and re-evaluate performance.

By completing these exercises, you'll gain practical experience in integrating Llama into real-world projects and develop a strong foundation for building successful applications.

Chapter 10: The Future of Llama: Trends and Advancements

Chapter 10.1: Introduction

The landscape of large language models is in a state of constant evolution. While we've explored the foundations and advanced techniques, the true potential of Llama and similar models lies in the uncharted territories of future development. This chapter will serve as a compass, guiding us through the emerging trends and potential breakthroughs that will shape the future of language models.

We'll delve into the exciting possibilities that lie ahead, from hardware advancements to groundbreaking architectural innovations. By understanding the direction of the field, we can position ourselves to contribute to and benefit from these developments.

Let's embark on this exploration of the future of Llama and the broader LLM landscape.

Chapter 10.2: Key Concepts

Hardware Acceleration

The relentless pursuit of faster and more efficient models has led to a focus on specialized hardware. Key developments include:

GPUs and TPUs: Continued advancements in these accelerators have significantly boosted training and inference speeds.

Specialized AI chips: Emerging hardware designed specifically for AI workloads.

Edge computing: Bringing AI capabilities closer to data sources for real-time applications.

Model Scaling

Increasing model size has shown impressive results, but it also comes with challenges:

Scaling laws: Understanding the relationship between model size, data, and performance.

Computational efficiency: Developing techniques to train and deploy larger models efficiently.

Overfitting prevention: Addressing the risk of overfitting as models grow larger.

Incorporating World Knowledge

Grounding language models in factual knowledge is crucial for accurate and informative responses:

Knowledge graphs: Integrating structured information into the model.

Retrieval-augmented generation: Combining information retrieval with language generation.

Factuality verification: Ensuring the accuracy of generated text.

Multimodality

Expanding beyond text to include other data formats opens up new possibilities:

Image, audio, and video integration: Enabling models to process and generate various media types.

Multimodal understanding: Developing models that can understand and generate content across different modalities.

Applications: Exploring new use cases such as image captioning, video summarization, and virtual assistants.

Explainable AI

Understanding the reasoning behind model decisions is essential for trust and accountability:

Attention visualization: Analyzing attention weights to understand model focus.

Feature importance: Identifying influential input features.

Counterfactual explanations: Understanding how changes in input affect the output.

These key concepts represent the forefront of LLM research, shaping the future of the field. By understanding these trends, you can anticipate the evolution of Llama and other language models.

Chapter 10.3: Hands-on Exercises (Exploratory)

Note: These exercises are exploratory in nature and may require significant computational resources and expertise.

Exercise 1: Experiment with Hardware Acceleration

Objective: Explore the impact of different hardware platforms on Llama performance.

Steps:

Train a Llama model on different hardware configurations (CPU, GPU, TPU).

Compare training and inference times.

Analyze the cost-benefit of using different hardware.

Exercise 2: Investigate Model Scaling

Objective: Explore the relationship between model size and performance.

Steps:

Train Llama models with different numbers of parameters.

Evaluate performance on benchmark datasets.

Analyze the trade-offs between model size, performance, and computational resources.

Exercise 3: Incorporate World Knowledge

Objective: Enhance Llama's knowledge base.

Steps:

Create a knowledge graph or database of relevant information.

Integrate the knowledge base into the Llama model.

Evaluate the model's ability to access and utilize world knowledge.

Exercise 4: Build a Basic Multimodal Model

Objective: Explore the potential of multimodal LLMs.

Steps:

Collect a dataset with text and image pairs.

Train a multimodal model to generate image descriptions or answer questions about images.

Evaluate the model's performance on a benchmark dataset.

Exercise 5: Analyze Model Explainability

Objective: Understand the decision-making process of a Llama model.

Steps:

Use attention visualization techniques to analyze model focus.

Experiment with feature importance methods.

Develop techniques to explain model predictions in human-understandable terms.

Note: These exercises are exploratory and may require significant computational resources and expertise. It's essential to approach these experiments with a focus on learning and experimentation rather than immediate results.